David
and
Goliath

Written by Sasha Morton
Illustrated by Alfredo Belli

Many years ago in Israel, there lived a boy named David who was the youngest of eight brothers. David spent his days quietly tending to his family's sheep and working as an armour-bearer for the king.

No one knew that David frightened off bears and lions that tried to attack his flock, using only his trusty slingshot. David may have been young, but he had very good aim.

Saul, the King of Israel, looked after his people well, but he was also very worried. Nearby, a huge army was waiting to fight his soldiers.

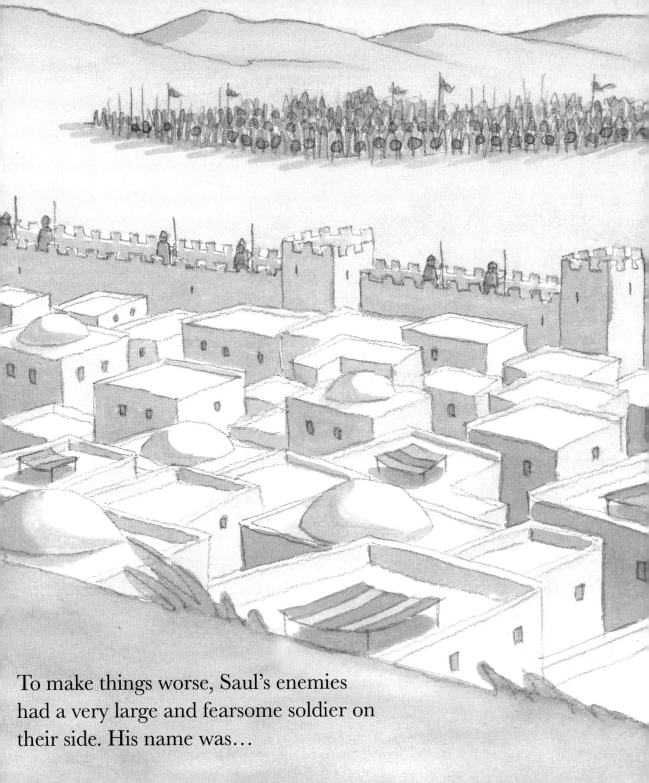

To make things worse, Saul's enemies
had a very large and fearsome soldier on
their side. His name was…

...GOLIATH!

Goliath towered over everyone around him and wore heavy metal armour. His spear was the size of a tree and wherever he walked, the land shook beneath his feet. He was terrifying!

"Send a man to fight me!" he roared to Saul's army.
But no one would go near him. Days passed and nobody
was strong enough to fight this enormous giant.

For forty days Goliath thundered onto the battlefield shouting, "Send a man to fight me! If he beats me, our people will be your slaves. If I defeat him, your people will become our servants."

Saul even offered a huge reward to
anybody who would fight Goliath,
but still nobody was brave enough to try.

One morning, Goliath stood between the
two armies and shouted his usual threat.

Saul's soldiers were terrified, but on this day, it just so happened that David was visiting his brothers in the army camp. David grew angry. He was fed up of hearing this giant insult his people, who worked hard and put their faith in God to protect them. It was time for someone to fight back!

David went to Saul and said,
"I, your servant, will fight this giant."

"David, you are only a boy, and Goliath has
been a warrior his entire life!" gasped the king.

"That may be," replied David. "But if God
can protect me while I keep my sheep safe, he will
protect me in a battle against this enemy too."

Everyone was shocked that David would even try to fight Goliath, but they helped get him ready for the battle.

Saul dressed David in his own golden armour and gave David his magnificent sword. However, when David tried to walk, he made a surprising discovery…

…he could not move! David took off the
shining armour and handed it back to Saul.

"What will you take to protect you?"
asked the worried king.

David held up his trusty slingshot. "Just this," he replied
firmly. David carefully chose five smooth stones from the
nearby riverbed. He tucked them into his shepherd's pouch,
and with only his sling in his hand, went to meet Goliath.

15

David took a deep breath and began to walk across the battlefield, where Goliath was waiting to fight. As he drew closer, Goliath began to laugh.

"You are the warrior that Saul has sent to fight me?" he bellowed in disbelief.

"You may raise a sword and a spear at me," David called up at him, "but I stand here in the name of the Lord."

With that, David slid a
stone into his sling…

…took aim

…and fired!

The smooth stone span through the air.

The soldiers on both sides gasped
and held their breath...

...and David's aim, as ever, was true.

The stone hit Goliath right in the forehead!
For a moment he stood completely still.

Then with a stagger,
a stumble and an almighty crash,
he fell down to the ground.

The enemy had been defeated!

Saul's soldiers chased their enemies out of Israel, and the whole land celebrated!

Even David's seven older brothers had to admit that they were proud of their quiet little brother.

David fought in many more battles and he always had faith that God would protect him. Many years later, David became the King of Israel, but he would always be remembered as the small boy who defeated a giant.

An Hachette UK Company
www.hachette.co.uk

First published in Great Britain in 2013 by TickTock,
an imprint of Octopus Publishing Group Ltd,
Endeavour House,
189 Shaftesbury Avenue,
London WC2H 8JY.

www.octopusbooks.co.uk

ISBN 978 1 84898 818 7

A CIP record of this book is available from the British Library

Printed and bound in China

1 3 5 7 10 8 6 4 2

With thanks to: Jana Burson

Series Editor: Lucy Cuthew   Design: Advocate Art
Publisher: Tim Cook   Managing Editor: Karen Rigden
Production: Lucy Carter